IN THE NAME OF GOD

Entrepreneurship as done by

Jalil Tavazo

The Founder of
Tavazo Nuts and Dried Fruits

Written by:
Dr. Reza Yadegari
Dr. Mahshid Sanaeefard
The Winners of the Prestigious
Jalal Al-e Ahmad Literary Award
and
Aryaan Yadegari
Lilyaan Yadegari
The Second Generation Authors of the
Great Iranian Entrepreneur Book Collection

Kidsocado Publishing House
Vancouver, Canada

Phone: +1 (833) 633 8654
WhatsApp: +1 (236) 333 7248
Email: info@kidsocado.com
https://kidsocadopublishinghouse.com
https:/kidsocado.com

Serial Number: P 2446190212
Title: Entrepreneurship as done by Jalil Tavazo
Sub Title: The Founder of Tavazo Nuts and Dried Fruits
Series Name: Iranian Great Entrepreneurs
Authors: Dr. Reza Yadegari, Dr. Mahshid Sanaeefard
Contributor Authors: Aryaan Yadegari, Lilyaan Yadegari
Copyist: Great Entrepreneur
ISBN: 978-1-77892-142-1
Metadata: Entrepreneurship/ Biography /Business & Economics
Book: Paperback
Pages: 54
Canada Publish Date: July 2024
Publisher: Kidsocado Publishing House

All Rights Reserved, including the right of production
in whole or part in any form.
Copyrigh@2024 by
Kidsocado Publishing House

- Introduction 3
- The Greenlight 5
- The life and world of Jalil Tavazo 7
- Interview with the third-generation Ali Tavazo 19
- The analysis of Tavazo Nuts and Dried Fruits 28
founder's success factors

Introduction

The work of identifying the greatest Iranian entrepreneurs got underway back in 1997 with the help and assistance of my wife Dr. Mahshid Sanaeefard, the Manager of the Great Iranian Entrepreneurs Publication. An exceptionally long and arduous task, which has enabled us to gain substantial insight into the world of entrepreneurship and job creation, and thus make history for the future generation of Iranians by helping found and chart a whole new path towards true success in business and industry alike.

Next to winning numerous international awards on this incredible journey of countless ups and downs, we have cooperated and collaborated extensively with some of Iran's highly accredited and most reputable higher learning centers, like Sharif Industrial University, University of Science and Technology, Alzahra University and Shahid Beheshti University. Moreover, we have also successfully established and registered the International Qualification and Certification Auditors Company or IQCA in Canada, whose main role and responsibility is to publish the life history of the greatest Iranian entrepreneurs to make them known by name to the other people in the world. IQCA has also been highly active in setting up and establishing an award presentation scheme in Iran in order to identify and introduce the country's most creative individuals and organizations, and thereby aid and assist with promoting them on a global scale.

It is hoped that as a special and leading group, we are able to introduce the most powerful Iranian women and me to the rest of the world and at the same time, identify and retell the life stories of the best role models for Iran's next generation.

Dr. Reza Yadegari
www.IBDC.ws

The Greenlight

The movement to transfer the experiences of the world's greatest entrepreneurs is one of the most important factors in helping the American and European companies and organizations' progress and improvement. These companies and organizations had concluded rather smartly that if a society wishes significant advancement and development, it must keep its eye on the experiences of the previous generation and not allow the young to incur costs on the system by experiencing and learning through trial and error. In line with the same notion, entrepreneurship has the potential to create notable transformation throughout a given society's various levels provided it is implemented using principles and plans that take advantage of the experiences of the proficient and skilled members. Allowing the young to take over across the world is certainly a commendable measure, which has also been taken in our beloved Iran as well, except that here the experiences of the previous generation of entrepreneurs and managers has never been made properly available for application by the new generation – something that has regrettably inflicted irrecoverable costs onto the country because of the continuous repetition of the same old mistakes. Our project to identify the greatest Iranian entrepreneurs, so that we may research their lives to understand the reasons and factors for their success started off back in 1997 simultaneously as the arrival of the novel science of entrepreneurship in Iran. Admittedly, the path has been a long one involving strenuous effort. In the years following the events of the Iranian Revolution, literary no entrepreneur in the country was willing to unveil and reveal herself or himself and the experiences she or he possessed.

In spite of this, we were quite determined to fulfil our goal of teaching and training the future generation by documenting and publishing the life stories and experiences of Iran's greatest entrepreneurs through a one-thousand-volume book aptly titled 'Entrepreneurship as done by …' What is presented in the book collection, is rare and valuable roadmap designed based on the experiences and performances of Iran's greatest economic minds, which undoubtedly can be a wonderful asset in guiding and directing anyone who intends to get involved in any type of commercial, production and service provision activity. We hope that our collection book can help open up doors and pave the way for Iran's new generation of young entrepreneurs, and also remain a lasting piece of literary work to remember us by.

Dr. Reza Yadegari
Dr. Mahshid Sanaeefard
Tehran, Iran 2024

The life and world of
Jalil Tavazo

The birth of the first nuts store
City of Tabriz (the capital city of East Azerbaijan Province, in northwestern Iran) has many neighborhoods, and Ahrab is just one of them. I was born in this neighborhood seventy five years ago or in 1936. My six siblings, namely three brothers and three sisters were also born in the same city and same neighborhood. My grandfather was one of Tabriz's biggest fruit farm owners and his large farms produced a wide variety of fruits such as apples, apricots, peaches, cherries, watermelons and cantaloupes. Although, our grandfather's fruit orchards yielded plenty of products, my father's perspective on life or horizon, if you will, was completely different from that of his father's. He was more interested in taking up a profession that would continue to grow and develop long into the future. To him farming was an extremely labor intensive job and quite often risky as crop yields varied dramatically from season to season depending on the amount of rainfall and other natural factors. Therefore, he

chose a business that despite being agriculturally-based processed fruits for convenient storage over a long period of time. Processing nuts was a relatively new method of preserving agricultural yields, which not only helped prolong the product life cycle, but also appealed to the taste of people and found more and more customers as the selection of the processed products in the market increased. My father began with grapes and peas. The fresh grapes would be neatly arranged on special platforms set up on scaffolds in the basement of his store and covered by tarp to prevent dust until they completely dried. Though, nitric acid, which could markedly speed up the drying process, was available then, my father never used the hazardous chemical because he cared about people's health. Drying the grapes naturally was extremely difficult and time-consuming, but he chose to use the organic method anyway. In addition to making raisins, he also processed peas to turn them into chickpeas. Since today's roasting equipment did not exist in those day yet, they would put the peas in large cooking vessels and use charcoal to heat and roast them. Once the raisins and chickpeas were ready, they would be placed inside large sacks and brought upstairs to the store to be sold. This was my father's daily work routine on most days and often until very late at nights. In time, he started processing more crops, which he either purchased from the farms in Tabriz or the other cities. Offering the customers high quality products was his only concern, so he would quite often bear the burden of going to faraway places just to find the best and finest products. Pretty soon a wide range of new processed goods like dried silverberry, and apricot, roasted hemp and sunflower seeds, pistachios, fava beans and corn kernels were added to the products at my father's store.

My childhood

Back in those days, each neighborhood in Tabriz had its own pre-school, where the children would typically start at the age of four by learning the Koran. So I was also sent to our local pre-school for a couple of years until I was six and ready to enter school as a first-grader. I really liked studying and being able to read and write. Though, I was poor at writing and dictation, I excelled at math and geometry and my marks in these two subjects were rarely less than 'A'. It was almost like I had a knack for math and geometry, and they came natural to me. The school that I went to had a very kind principal and some really wonderful and skilled teachers, who taught most everything in Azari (the name used for the Iranian language composed of groups of dialects spoken in Azerbaijan in northwest region of Iran).

An eight-year-old nut seller

Familiarizing their children with the culture of working and earning an honest living is one of the most important traits of people in Tabriz. Perhaps, breathing the spirit of perseverance and due diligence into the children early on in life is the reason why the region has produced some of the country's most prominent merchants and businesspeople. So I began working at my father's store as soon as I turned eight. He assigned the duty of roasting the nuts to me, and I used to do whatever within my power to help lift some of the enormous weight off this hard working man's shoulders. I would get up at four in the morning and go to the store and clean and tidy things up a bit until about eight when I would head to school. Our lunch break was from 12:00 to 2:00 PM, but I would even use that time to help my father. Again, once the school ended at four o'clock, I'd grab my things and get back to the store as quickly as I could and work until ten or eleven o'clock at night. My father worked alone and had no help. Since he could neither read nor write, he really relied on me with the books and the accounts. Indeed, his regular compliments, particularly in front of the other people warmed my heart and served as a great motivational factor to perform my tasks and duties to the best of my ability.

My future profession

After the end of sixth grade, when I was about fifteen or so, I decided to quit school and work alongside my brothers to help our father. I was in charge of production and sales. We were buying our supplies from anyplace across Iran that produced first-grade agricultural goods. Everything used to be cleaned and prepared early in the mornings, and then roasted for sales during the day. In spite of the simple life that most people lived and their limited earnings, our nut store was almost always packed and we used to sell a lot every day. We also lived a pretty average life and what we made was just enough to make ends meet. Unlike today, when people buy large quantities of nuts, back then people could only afford to buy enough for personal use and as a result, our revenue was limited and we had to constantly work to produce more goods.

My intellectual father

Despite lacking formal education, my father had a world of experience and working next to him was like going to a life-lesson university every day. He was firm and determined in making sure that his children learnt the proper way of living. At mealtimes, he always spoke in a kind, gentle voice about doing the right thing and loving and respecting others. He was an intelligent man whose wise words broadened his children's horizons. My father believed in and practiced customer-orientation and valued and respected his customers. He was quite hopeful about the future of nuts and always used to say that the business would grow and flourish greatly one day. He was a devout man, who emphasized on honesty and making a clean living by offering customers the highest quality products. I remember when we bought a bunch of large, Russian-made crystal bowls for the store; he turned to me and said, "Look Jalil, nuts will become very popular someday." And when I inquired the reason, he replied, "You see these crystal bowls filled with nuts if we continue to produce first-rate products and display and package them nicely, we're going to make our business grow rapidly." Looking at the global nut and dried fruit industry nowadays, I realize that my old man was absolutely right. Today, our products are no longer for personal consumption only, and they are being exported to many countries around the world.

The day when I married

Our lives continued pretty much the same way as my brothers and I worked right alongside our father. He had brought us up in a way that we completely understood expenses, assets and liabilities, or in other words, managing finances. If we happened to be pressed for money, we could take however much we needed from the store's cash box. He used to caution us all the time about spending our money wisely and not forgetting to save for a rainy day. This kind of upbringing was the reason that my brothers and I watched our hard-earned money very closely. In any event, our father was never too strict about financial matters and had absolute faith in us. My mother was a virtuous and caring lady, who did splendidly well in raising my siblings and I. By the time I reached twenty seven, my younger brother had already married, but I was still single. So, based on what was customary then, she rolled up the sleeves and got busy going around checking with friends and acquaintances to find a nice wife for her son. When she finally did find the right 'match,' I accepted immediately since I had absolute trust in her ability and good taste. Without a doubt, my marriage has been a very successful one, and I have always been satisfied and happy. For the first couple of years, my wife and I lived at my father's house. And in the blink of an eye, we were blessed with two daughters and a son.

The day when dear father departed for his eternal home and left us alone

Investing his money in the best possible manner was one of our father's best qualities. He used most of what he had labored for all those years to buy real estate since he believed that because of the rising prices, land and buildings could have a promising future. I also took some of my savings on the same premises to buy a store on one of Tabriz's main streets, so that I could have something for the future. I worked with my father and brothers for over thirty eight years or up to the time when our dear father passed away at the age of ninety five. After his death, my brothers and I ran his store together for another fifteen years. By then, Tavazo nuts, which we had registered under the name 'The Original Tavazo,' had become extremely popular and famous. As a matter of fact, the nuts and dried fruits produced and sold at our store were unrivaled in the country, and we were undoubtedly one of the industry's main contenders. The precious experiences gained from our grandfather and father had taught us that working together and supporting each other was the only way to succeed. That's why we never permitted trivia and insignificant matters to cause problems in our partnership.

My son and I start our own independent store

My son was getting closer to the working age, and I really wanted to see him work just like I had done so many years before. So I turned our father's store over to my younger brother, who incidentally is still running the business there and doing a fantastic job at it too, so that my son and I could start running our own business. We managed to stand on our own feet in almost no time at all and as the work conditions improved, we decided that it was about time that we apply the wealth of experience we had accumulated over the years in order to nurture and expand our operations even further. One of the measures that we took on par with this notion was the addition of extra goods to our inventory as we followed every principle ever learned from my father to a tee.

Opening up the Tehran branch

Time was moving fast as days turned into nights and nights into days. I was so caught up in my work that I completely missed out on how quickly my daughters had grown up grew up and reached the marriage age. As it often happens when people marry, our daughters had to move to Tehran, where their husbands lived and worked. The far distance and the separation from her daughters to whom she was very much attached took a serious toll on my wife, so much so that she fell ill. So I had no choice but to send her to live in the Capital too. Pretty soon, she and my son were insisting that I buy a store in Tehran, where they believed we could increase our revenue by ten times in comparison to Tabriz. Though, I really didn't like to risk everything, I finally gave in to the unbearable pain of being away from my family and decided to move. After settling into our new home and getting used to life in a new place somewhat, we began searching the City for a nice location to open up our store. Since

I believed that in the beginning, we had to start off somewhere quiet, which had not undergone much development; we were mainly looking at the less crowded areas of Tehran. The location that we finally picked was exactly such a place. Despite being kind of far from the inner areas of the City at the time and being surrounded by fruit farms, which gave the impressions of a countryside rather than part of an urban center, I was confident that it had plenty of room for future growth. The store's grand opening, received a pretty warm welcome and soon sales were soaring so high that we had to have truckloads of nuts delivered from Tabriz on daily basis. At first, all goods were displayed in the same sacks they were delivered in. But because of our unique customer-orientation approach and excellent public relations, we listened to our customers' recommendations on merchandise display and built several glass displays and purchased a bunch of elegantly designed crystal vessels to aesthetically exhibit and offer our high-quality nuts and dried fruits. My wife used to come to the store in her spare time too and give us novel ideas on the floor layout and arrangement of goods. As a matter of fact, the addition of saffron to the store's inventory was her suggestion. The decoration work definitely required a female's touch, and she along with her insight and fantastic taste soon turned into a great asset for the business. Indeed, I dare to admit that I truly owe a huge part of my success to her. Though, we had also dedicated a part of the store to a storing goods and roasting and packaging nuts, we were selling so much that the space could no longer support our operations, and we had to find a larger place to accommodate our needs. This was the reason why we opened the Tavazo Nuts Factory in Karaj (capital of Alborz Province, Iran, and effectively a suburb of Tehran), where today forty to forty five workers clean, roast, package and store nuts.

The Original Tavazo Nuts

Just like most other successful businesses, which fall victim to copyright infringements, Tavazo faced the same ordeal. So we selected 'The Original Tavazo' as our trademark and registered it immediately to prevent people from illegally imitating our products. At the present time, we have three separate branches, where over hundred fifty personnel work full-time under my son's direct supervision. We have also begun exporting our merchandise abroad for the past several years. In addition, many local merchants buy our products, and then export them to countries in Africa and many others across the world like the United States, New Zealand, Germany, Spain and Italy. People love our goods in America and Europe because of their exceptionally fine quality and one-of-a-kind taste. This is particularly true with our walnuts, which simply cannot be rivalled anywhere in the world. Needless to say that the other countries have their own special nuts; however, their texture and taste is not nearly as good as Iran's. The special taste and grade quality have increased Iran's share of roasted nuts and dried fruit export drastically – something that we most certainly take pride and joy in.

The world's best nuts!

Today, I can claim that quality nuts produced by 'Haj Jalil Tavazo and Son' are unequivocally and indisputably the best anywhere in the world. Many factors have had a part in Tavazo Nuts ultimate success, but I think of my son's role as the most effective of all. His hard work and above extraordinary demeanor next to his excellent management have constantly added to our strings of success. As the old saying goes, 'What you put out is what you get.' I believe this to be certainly true about my family. When my father needed me, I put out for him with all my might. And now, it is my son, who is giving me and our business all that he's got. Achieving the level of success that Tavazo Nuts has enjoyed over the past several decades has not come easy, and it took an enormous amount of constant work and perseverance as well as correct thinking and investing coupled with the biggest factor; patience. I believe that the accumulation of wealth is done correctly and appropriately when the fulfillment of the Almighty God's wishes and expectations are taken into consideration. Consistently, when the work is carried out in earnest and people are given the highest grade products, the business begins to develop and sales figures start to climb. In all honesty, I do think that whatever I happen to have today is owed to my father. In the final days of his life, he told me time and again about the importance of maintaining a favorable public image by doing good deeds and serving the people to live honorably. He advised me to always follow three things in business to remain successful: Never accept a post-dated check, never sign anything before reading it and never guarantee anyone. "You won't lose any sleep at nights if you think about your work's quality and prosperity and understand your limit," he said. I recommend to the young to either learn their father's work if possible or to go after a specific type of profession or industry. Also, use perseverance and due diligence in whatever you start and cut down on your leisure time to generate feasible results and outcomes. Hanging out with friends is fun. But too much of it can waste a big chunk of your best years. Keeping the mind on work is one of the secrets to success. When the mind is engaged and focused on work, it can lead to innovative creativity and presentation of new ways to raise product quality. In the end, I like to wish all Iranians, especially the young health, longevity and success."

Interview with the third generation Ali Tavazo

Similar to Haj Ali Tavazo, who emphasized greatly on raising his children to the best of his ability and as he saw fit, Jalil Tavazo also applied his excellent management and keen sense of providence to transfer all of his learnings and skills onto his son: Ali Tavazo. By using the experiences of the previous generations, proper planning and continuous performance upgrading to surpass the local market and enter global domains, the Tavazos' family-run business is a true to life example of grand entrepreneurship. What you are about to read is an interview with Tavazo Nuts and Dried Fruits' young manager or Ali Tavazo meant as a complement to his father's life story and years of valuable experiences.

- **When was 'Tavazo Nuts and Dried Fruits' born?**
• Nuts and Dried Fruits was founded about a hundred twenty years ago in a small store owned by my grandfather 'Haj Ali Tavazo' in the City of Tabriz. The store is still open and operating under my uncle's management.
- **How did your grandfather start his work in that small store?**
• Well, he began with only two or three merchandise. He used

to dry grapes to make raisins, which he would then mix in with his specially roasted chickpeas to sell in his store. After a couple of years, he started selling walnuts and almonds too.

- How many different types of nuts are currently sold by Tavazo stores?

• Right now, we have an assortment of over three hundred types of nuts, which are processed and packaged using fully-automated systems.

- What do you suppose is the reason for Tavazo's remarkable success?

• In my opinion, the careful and thorough attention that my grandfather and father paid to their work was the first reason. Their constant presence in the store enabled them to understand the customers' needs and interests, so they could work on eliminating anything that could lead to customer dissatisfaction. The second reason was their passion and moral and ethical approach to their work.

- How have your grandfather, father and you been able to pass on this sympathetic and moral view onto the customers?

• Allowing the customers to taste the products at our stores for free before buying anything is one of the techniques. What's more Tavazo owned business and has never used any kind of public funding. And basically everything we have used to develop and expand our business has been made possible by the people.

- How did Tavazo end up coming to Tehran and found its way among the people there?

• Well, my dad bought his first store in Tehran in 1989. At the time, no other nuts producer was offering their products in modern packaging – something that certainly increased to Tavazo's popularity and rapid development.

- How many people used to work at the Tehran branch at the onset?

• At first, we used to have only four employees. But we have one hundred fifty, forty of whom work at the factory, and the remaining one hundred ten work at our different stores.

- MR. Tavazo, why are you and your father always seen working alongside your employees?

• Because our line of work requires us to be in constant contact with the customers just in case there is any problem. At the same time, our presence is also a sign of courtesy and respect toward our valued customers, which in a way is a form of marketing as well and keeping up with market's pulse. In my opinion, no one can do your job better than you can.

- Are your personnel as faithful to you as you are to your customers?

• Well, nothing is always one hundred percent, and you always have to leave a little room, or maybe even more than a little, for miscalculations. But I can tell you with certainty that ninety nine percent are. We have one employee by the name of Akbar Ghasemi, who's been working at our Tabriz store for over fifty years. I think this is proof of loyalty, and the fact that the employer has kept its employee happy in every way.

- How many branches does Tavazo have throughout the

country?

• Ever since 2001, when we started to expand our operations, we've been able to establish twelve different branches four of which are right here in Tehran.

- **Do you accept authorized agents and how?**

• Anyone applying for an authorized sales and distribution center must have at least worked in the nuts business for at least six months. They can buy from us in bulk, and sell their merchandise at a slightly higher price. The license is valid for one year, but renewable if there are no complications. In reality, the assignment of our brand has a spiritual value or meaning to us because only the licensed agency makes a profit and not us. Our sole aim and intention is to develop Tavazo's name and not profitability.

- **Do you keep track of your monthly deliveries and do you have an exact number?**

• It's difficult to give an exact figure because our sales are season-dependent.

- **Many would like to be in your position. What is your real feeling about your station?**

• The position is greatly owed to the last two generations of Tavazo. So I feel now that I have do my duties as best as possible to live up to our family name and honor. And, of course, this trend has to continue after me too.

- **What is so special about Tavazo's nuts that make them so popular?**

• Well, the quality is the first and foremost. The next is the availability of our goods. We always have what the customers want and as much as they want. Therefore, the phrase 'No, we don't have any' has no meaning at Tavazo.

- **Where do you buy your supplies?**

• The nuts and dried fruits are actually the pick of the crops at the places across the country famous for what we buy. But no matter where our supplies come from, they are all processed at our factory in Karaj.

- **Considering the long history of your business enterprise, do you also appeal to the taste of the new generations of customers too?**

• Our customers are from three different generations just like us, meaning that the grandfathers used to be my grandfather's customers while the fathers were my dad's and the sons are now mine. Also, we've always had a large number of tourist customers, particularly from 1991 to 2005.

- **Has the generation gap between you and your father led to any management issues?**

• Yes because my father prefers the traditional method of management while I prefer the new version. So we've had our share of challenges. Actually, the difference of opinion or taste, if you will, is one of the reasons preventing our operations to become completely mechanized. For example, I have always believed that our packaging and the way we supply our products must be diverse and up-to-date. But my father opposes the idea. I also like to have the customers be served in turns based on a number that we give them. But again, my dad is totally against the idea. Who knows? Maybe when I'm his age, I think the same way.

- **Have you ever had any competitors that surpassed you?**
  • Well, there is plenty of competition in our line of work. And some of them perhaps sell more than we do. But our activities are different.

- **Does Tavazo sell products in different packages?**
  • We have one store at Imam Khomeini Airport that offers our goods in exclusive packages. And its sales numbers are pretty decent.

- **Which brands are the most successful after yours?**
  • There are several like Ayoob, Nahal-e Rafsanjan Pistachios, Mani and Fard.

- **Since Tavazo has already positioned itself in the market so well, why don't you give its management to a group of educated and knowledgeable individuals?**
  • Well unlike most businesses, ours is not the kind that needs to necessarily rely on education, particularly given the fact that our management method is experience-based.

- **Has there been a year when your sales were extraordinarily high?**
  • Yes in 1997 when the Islamic Summit was being held in Tehran. We've noticed that different cultures have different habits of shopping. For example, the Arabs usually buy the most, meaning if they point to a package of some product, they literally mean the entire shelf. But the Europeans tend to buy only as much as they need for personal use.

- **What's the best way to store and keep nuts at home?**
  • Nuts should be placed in a sealed plastic bag and kept in

the fridge in temperatures of to 7°C to 15°C. However, nuts should never be kept in the freezer since freezing affects the nuts' quality and taste significantly. The reason that I recommended airtight plastic is to keep the moisture.

- **Is there any way to get rid of nuts' musty smell?**

• Unfortunately not. The musty smell is caused by an irreversible chemical process, which affects both the quality and taste.

- **How is the quality and price of the nuts sold by the street vendors as compared to the shops?**

• The street vendors don't have any overhead costs so they can afford to sell their goods at lower prices, which are typically ten to twenty percent less than the stores' prices. One thing that is very important is the amount and even balance of salt in the final product. The salt content of the nuts sold in the streets is often high, which means the customer is actually paying for salt. The quality varies greatly as well. For example, the pistachios could of the finest grade, but you can count about ten or so out of a handful with closed shells. Another issue with regards to the nuts sold by the street vendors that's worth mentioning is the unhygienic conditions. There are all kinds of pollution in the urban centers, which the nuts sold in open-top containers or sacks in the streets are exposed to.

- **What is the salt content or percentage of the standard products?**

• According the standards specified by the Ministry of Health, we can only add about three percent salt to the products during the processing phase. Of course, certain types of nuts like the 'Arabian' or 'Indian' nuts are a little saltier.

- **Don't you think that the nut prices in Tehran are a bit too high? And are the prices affected by the customers' taste and vary from one part of the City to another?**
  • Well, the prices go up by ten to twenty percent each year regardless of the elements that you mentioned. In addition, the currency exchange fluctuation, which impacts nearly everything in the domestic market, affects the prices of different nuts too.
- **When do you normally prepare the nuts that are used for Yalda (Shab-e Yalda is an ancient winter solstice festival celebrated by the Iranians on the longest and darkest night of the year on or about December 21st) and the Persian New Year?**
  • We usually start preparing the products in the latter days of November, and most people start buying what they need beginning the second week of December. On average, our sales are tens time higher during those special times of the year.
- **Isn't the end of November a little too soon?**
  • Not really because some of our customers want to send nuts to their friends and relatives living abroad, so we have to have the nuts ready in a timely manner to leave enough time for shipping.
- **Do the nuts shipped abroad reach the recipients intact?**
  • Yes if they are wrapped and packaged properly. We actually accept orders for customized packaging in special boxes, bags and pouches too if the customer requests it.
- **Do the customers often need your workers' assistance or do they always know how much nuts they want?**
  • Yes, sometimes they'd like to know how much nuts is enough

for a certain number of guests. We typically recommend one hundred grams per guest.

- **What are the main ingredients of the nuts that are prepared for Shab-e Yalda?**
• We use raw or unprocessed pistachios, two types of raisins, walnuts, almonds, dried figs and apricots. Of course, I have to point out that there's wide variety and selection of nuts with each one often having several subclasses of its own. For example, price of raisins changes depending on whether or not they are seedless. The same is true with the other dried fruits. Their prices change depending on the type of processing. Like pineapple, which could be processed in chunks or rings, or be naturally sweet or sweetened using sweeteners. We purchase more than seventy percent of our supplies such as pistachios, walnuts, raisins, plums, barberry, etc. from the domestic suppliers. But we export some items like cranberry from Canada, and also cashew, which is not found locally, from India and Africa.

- **Cashew did not exist in Iran in the past?**
• No, it was quite rare. Prior to the 1990s, it was basically what the travelers brought as souvenir for friends and family. But cashew exports began around that time and today cashews can be found almost anywhere in the country.

- **What did you major in?**
• I majored in computer software. But I chose to follow in my forefathers' footsteps and do the same thing that my father Jalil, my grandfather Ali and my great-grandfather Yousef started in Tabriz so many years ago.

The analysis of Tavazo Nuts and Dried Fruits founder's success factors

The close examination of the lives of Iran's greatest entrepreneurs reveals valuable points, which have gone unheeded for the most part and haven't really gotten the recognition and credit that they are so rightfully worthy of. The wealth of experiences that these women and men have accumulated throughout the years based on their customers' social behaviors, public policies, stable and permanent occupations' trends as well as a host of other elements can aid and assist in opening up new doors to a large degree for anyone intending to enter the world of entrepreneurship more quickly. Similarly, the experience and practical wisdom gained by the Tavazos through years of running their family-owned business are among some of the most precious generational knowledge and mastery ever attained by anyone. The family, known and praised for its professional maintenance of a favorable public image and kind-hearted and considerate treatment of their customers, has in many instances observed the ethical codes of professionalism and good business practice without any first-hand knowledge of the respective scientific standards and criteria. This is, indeed, the reason that their good name and honor has withstood the test of time from generation to generation and today, is stronger than at any time in the past. What follows next is the basis of the Tavazo family's entrepreneurship approaches and insights, whose close and critical application can prove beneficial and advantageous for any business establishment.

Put together and prepare a complete business plan before getting started

The preparation of a thorough and comprehensive business plan could turn out to be one of the most difficult things to do if you wish to start up a successful business. The most accomplished entrepreneurs spend weeks and sometimes months to put together a suitable one prior to getting their business started. Fortunately, there are different types of software available in the market today that can be wonderful tools to help you outline a suitable business plan. But, you must create the business plan on your own, and cannot get someone else to do it for you. The number one advantage of having such a plan is that it enables you to assess and measure the business' every single component. For instance, the quantity or volume of the products or services that will be sold monthly or annually within the next three years, or the costs and expenses involving the production and distribution of these products and services from the standpoint of the location, facilities, tools and equipment, advertisements and employees or anything else that may be required. The business plan will also make it possible for you to project your potential profits in the years to come. Of course, you need to bear in mind the two important rules as well. First, everything will cost twice what you figured and second, everything will take three times longer than you estimated. Once the business plan is ready, you can show it to knowledgeable and experienced people to get their opinion and consultation. Be prepared to use their feedback and new information to make the necessary modifications and corrections. The very same way that a final drawing is needed for constructing a building, after completion, a business plan forms the basis for building your enterprise. And helps you later on to navigate the turbulent waters of the business world.

Prevent the mistakes that lead to a business failure and defeat

The results and conclusions of countless surveys conducted by the large accounting and consultation firms indicate that some factors leading to business failure are common and alike. So beware and cleverly avoid every single one. Not having a specific orientation or direction is thought to be the first reason that most businesses fail. What this means is that the business has no specific goals for each part of the work throughout a given day. This is usually because the company has not prepared a comprehensive business plan before starting-up. Impatience is the second reason for defeat in economic-based activities. Many companies try to gain the most in the least amount of time by, for example, spending a huge amount of money on advertising when they should be developing their operations step at a time as they address and cater to the customers' demands and requirements. Thus, it is important to remember the golden rule that 'everything will cost twice as much and take three times longer than what you had originally expected and counted on.' Greed is the third reason for failure in business. To sell a lot of products make a bunch of money fast without caring about establishing reputability first, many companies often resort to overpricing or charging too high a price for their products. Whereas, the best way is to start off with settling for reasonable profitability, and then increasing the prices in proportion to rise in demands. The fourth reason for failing businesses has to do with weak cost control schemes, especially at the onset of work. You have to remember that money is everything, and you need to maintain it at any cost; otherwise, when money is gone, the company is bound to follow next. Poor-quality products and services are the fifth reason leading to a company's defeat. Offering low-grade products and services makes things hard the first time and nearly impossible the second time. When quality is low, it is literally impossible to even make back the money that you paid for the things you bought. The sixth reason for failing is related to insufficient capital. Companies that run into this problem, haven't allocated a big enough budget, and therefore, run out of money. This is exactly why a business plan is absolutely essential. And finally for the seventh reason, which has to do with inadequate sales and the drop in the sales' units' pace. People often get so caught up in their work that they often tend to forget that nothing can go on and be done without selling. So, you have to concentrate a good deal on sales and give it priority over all the other activities.

Marketing; An entrepreneur's most important art

Immaterial of how you tend the various aspects of your business, it simply cannot succeed unless it can sell its products. This makes customer demand an extremely crucial factor to the success of any business. Indeed, the sheer existence of your business depends on the level of customers' satisfaction regarding your company's products and services. Therefore, you have to identify and understand their demands, and then develop your product and services to address and meet them. Of course, most small businesses don't have the necessary means, and thus they cannot allocate and spend large sums of money on developing their products' market. There are those entrepreneurs that have started up theirs businesses by either making a novel product or because of their deep personal passion and interest in the work. However, this is not a very smart way to begin. Perhaps, they were under the wrong impression that the customers would love their product or services. In any event, this is a wrong approach for an entrepreneur since creating demand requires investing a great deal of time, money and energy. If your business is about to enter the existing market most of your effort and capital is going to be devoted to and spent on finding new markets and promoting the customers to change their shopping habits in order to buy from you instead of the competition. Your products and services need to facilitate convenience for the customer. The market share that any business is able to take is proportional to its size. And it is literally impossible to own the entire market. So you have to concentrate on a specific part of the market, or in other words, the customer's special needs and demands, which may be classified based on categories such as income, geographical region, gender, age and taste and interest. Since the entire livelihood of your business depends on the customers, you must base your entire efforts on their demands. The trends and patterns described below will help you to identify the customer's behavioral changes.

- The rate of sales to the customer is the most significant index in determining success. Compare this month's sales to the previous year's and keep an eye open for any slumps that could be indicating the start of a negative trend.

- Pay particular attention to drop in credit sales the regular customers or the reduction of the number of new customers. If you notice any issues, talk to your staff members and customers, so that you may troubleshoot and eliminate the root causes.

- Since increased number of contacts with the customers to sell may not severely impact the sales figures, the sales people have to identify where the problems lies.

- Returned goods may be increasing, so make enquired with your staff and customers to find out why.

Do underestimate and ignore the change in the customers' behavior regarding your products too easily and get busy immediately to change the unfavorable trend that is causing the slump in sales. Many cannot afford the necessary research and development prior to launching their product. Therefore, because of the high cost of marketing, you most definitely have to ascertain whether or not you have the necessary means to launch your product and keep it afloat while you continue to do marketing. Majority of businesses have access to obliged financial resources and cannot afford to do both. Accordingly, production costs of a new product and its subsequent marketing expenses need to be kept to bare minimum. One of the things that you can do in this regard is to concentrate on the customer demands that the current market isn't meeting. While small businesses have their share of weaknesses, but their ability to adapt and conform to the changes in the market is certainly their distinct strength. Flexibility is a pretty useful tool to react to change in customer demand. A smart move is to be selective while maintaining favorable relationships with the customers to find out why they have stopped buying from you. Though, the continuous launch of new products and services is not possible for the small-scale businesses, they can turn to innovation in their production process or distribution system to compete with the big time players.

Pricing

Price is not the only determinant which decisively affects the nature or outcome sales and other factors such as personal attention, giving out complimentary product samples, credit sales and product diversity can also give you an edge over the competition. Make sure that all parts of your business - including the entire staff members - are customer-oriented. Conduct cyclical assessments of your relationships with the customers in order to identify any areas that may need improvement in order to increase sales. Pricing has to be done in such a way so as to cover the costs, and at the same time generate a reasonable profit. Notwithstanding, there are other considerations that have to be paid close attention to in this calculation. For instance, in cases where the competing power is limited or a unique product or line of services is being offered, pricing could become problematic since it may have little or no relation to the production costs and be calculated merely based on customer's demands. In most cases, limited competition tends to reduce your ability to price your goods properly. Pricing turns into an extremely important factor, when your products and services closely resemble that of the competition. Therefore, try to base the prices on the special features of your product. Believe in the motto: 'The Customer Is Always Right' and do your best to understand the customers and show interest in them. Remember that customers buy from a place where they are welcomed and feel that their needs are met.

Attracting new customers

The small businesses may not necessarily have to spend large sums of money on advertisements. since they mostly sell their products through personal contacts within the targeted segment of the population. Recommendation by satisfied customers is really vital, so ask them to introduce and recommend you to others or give you the names of those that may be interested in using your product or services. Moreover, your business must have its own individual trademark, which has to be printed on all the company's signs, business cards, invokes, letterheads, vehicles, delivery trucks, etc. What's more, the staff can also help identify new customers. They need to realize that their work depends on the company's success and higher sales figures actually guarantee their long-term job security. A clever entrepreneur uses different social activities to establish fruitful contacts with new customers. People tend to value and praise anything done for the community's sake, so they may decide to become your customer just to show their appreciation for your good deed. The advertisements, which target potential customers are usually quite expensive and hardly worth the cost. Therefore, radio and television commercials need to be carried out on a lesser scale first in order to determine whether or not they actually increase sales and are worth spending more money on. Flyers and direct mail advertising are other effective ways to get your message across. Since advertisements represent your business, any method you use to advertise your product or services must be attractive and appealing. In short, don't wait for the customers to come to you and go out and find them yourself.

Advertising the business

You are the key character in any advertisement and responsible for creating the positive business-public relationship. Generally, a business's fame and popularity is directly connected to the personality and actions of its owner or the entrepreneur. Identify the special customers, so that you can introduce your product and services to them through special adverts. Customers will certainly satisfy most of their needs and requirements through you if they trust your business. Advertising includes the set of 'special efforts' aimed at increasing the sales. Accordingly, ads may be in the form of a suggestion to introduce goods or services, discounts, special displays or free samples. To carry out a successful advertising campaign, you first have to have a proper understanding of the market that you are trying to reach. Identify the customers' demography and figure out who your customers are, where they come from and why they buy from you. Know your exact sales' rate at the present time and avoid advertising the same way that your main competitors do. Furthermore, pay particular attention to the other businesses' ads, especially the ones that affect your work and always remember that the customers' real demands are the basis for your advertisement schemes.

The sales advertising chart

Type of Ad	Cost of Ad"	Date of Ad	Sales during Advertising	Previous year's Sales
1-				
2-				
3-				

Once you have identified the potential market, you need to determine the type of advertising you intend to do. Keep the customers' main reasons for buying when you are making decision on which factors to advertise. Why do people shop? Because: (A) They are seeking distinction (new fashion or furniture, (B) They want to meet and satisfy their basic needs (food, housing), (C) They are interested in the non-essentials (new television, cosmetic), (D) They need products for their business (printer, work desk, vehicle). Your answers to the following questions will determine the type and scope of your sales advertisements:

- What are your marketing policies?
- What are your potential markets?
- What is your target group?
- Which medium should be use for advertising?
- Do you have enough money for seeing your advertising campaign through successfully?
- When should the sales advertisement start?
- How can the results and outcomes of the sales advertisements be assessed?
- What is the difference between your special advertisement and the other regular adverts?
- How involved are your staff members in the advertising campaign?
- Do the ads cover other products and services next to introducing the business?
- How can the effect of the ads be measured?

There are several other factors that have to be considered when deciding on the degree of the advertisement campaign. For example, if you've been running a successful business for a while, you probably won't need any kind special sales ads. However, if your business has recently changed locations, you need to run special ads to introduce yourself to the potential customers in the new area. In addition, your product also has a part in determining the right advertisements. Consistently, the more specialized your product, the more important the ads. The same thing is also true about location. So if you happen to be far from your customers, you have to do more advertising to reach them. Compare the sales figures before and after your advertisements in order to measure to figure out if your ads have generated the desired outcome. As any business grows, its respective market also has to be developed and expanded and special sales ad campaigns can be a great asset in this regard.

Advertisements

Though, advertisements attract and help the customer to willingly buy your product, it is really the product and service quality that determines whether or not the customer will return again. Most sales are ordinarily to the regular customers, so ads are not only meant for finding new customers, and they can also aid the old customers to remain up-to-date with respect to the latest developments in your business.

Print ads

Since the majority of ads are printed, it is important to know

their special characteristics:
- Print ads must be unique.
- They need to be simple and easy to understand.
- They have to contain useful information that dictate a main point.
- Finally, print ads must display a positive image of the enterprise.

Most businesses turn to their personnel to generate ideas that can be used to make ads instead of going to ad agencies. Don't forget that advertisements need to fit in well and be to the point. Many people read the newspapers to get information on special sales, so local papers are a pretty good medium for the small businesses. Moreover, the radio or television station, which is going to broadcast your ad, could help you prepare it.

Advertising's result assessment

Since advertising is quite costly, the business has to use it to produce the most effective result. Conducting a research is one useful way of measuring the rate of success. To maximize the ad's impact while minimizing the cost, determine a specific target group and use a special medium. Indeed, what is really important is not the amount of money, but how it is spent. A successful ad is one which increases sales to a degree so as to compensate for the cost of making it.

Creating awareness

A large number of entrepreneurs do not advertise simply because they lack the time and the necessary skill to see the ad campaign through. Because enterprises specialize in production rather than marketing, they need external help for their advertising. Advertisement campaigns have interwoven components, which must be coordinated and pointed to the right direction. This is exactly what an ad agency does. They provide the actors, designers and specialists, all of whom have their own special rates and perform all the other necessary responsibilities like planning, organizing, executing and assessing the entire ad campaign process. When looking for an ad agency, try finding one that specializes in your particular kind of market immaterial of whether you are a retailer, a wholesaler or an industry. You should also check with the intended ad agency's former customers to get their feedback, and also review the agency's previous performance and ask about the any questionable cost and make sure it can be justified. Many advertisement agencies have contracts with the publications as well as the radio and television stations and receive special discounts. So as the frequency of your ads increases, you may want to hire an advertising expert to establish a more direct control on your ad campaign. Advertisements are normally a fixed part of any business, so make sure that each advertising stage is in total coordination with your comprehensive plans. Certain businesses, particularly the ones involving consumables can also use suppliers to advertise their goods. As a general rule, advertising is the best way to attract the potential customers, but once you do, it is you and your staff's job to turn them into your enterprise's regular customers.

Grant of rights

Businesses grant rights in order to have their products or services distributed through authorized sales centers. This is one area of trade and commerce that is undergoing remarkable growth. Grant of rights makes it possible for the concessionaire to market its products or services based on special terms and provisions. Indeed, assignment of rights is one of the ways, which most certainly can lead to the business' rapid growth and development. When assigning rights, you may have to grant the following options to the assignee:

- The choice to select and purchase the most ideal location.
- The choice to construct the required building to suit the distribution and sales operations.
- Accessibility to financial resources.
- The utilization of the standard trends and procedures corresponding to the business' various aspects such as accounting, management and production.

The people that you grant rights to may inquire into why operating under your license is better than starting up a new business, so you need to satisfactory answers for them.

The product survey

- What is the projected market for your product?
- Who are your main competitors?
- How comparable is your product to the similar products?
- Is your product just a fad or will it have long-term demand?

The concession agreement

- Is the agreement fair to both parties?
- Is the agreement comprehensive enough? And have all the business aspects been taken into consideration by its respective terms and provisions?
- Are the conditions for buying the concession license reasonable?
- Are the agreement's terms and provisions exclusive? Particularly as they pertain to: (A) fixed payments, (B) goods purchase agreements, (C) sales shares, (D) exclusive rights, (E) agreement renew options, (F) agreement's expiration and termination and (G) the entire costs involving the grant of right.

The concessionaire's aid and assistance

- What type of training is available to the management and the staff?
- What are the existing special warehouse inventory control procedures?
- What kinds of marketing survey and assessment have been conducted?
- What are the conditions of the advertisements and promotions being considered for the special sales campaigns?
- What kind of financial aid is available?

The market backgrounds

- How wide is the concession catering market?

- Is the market domain widespread enough to support the grant of rights?
- What are the profitability experiences in the other concession domains?
- Do the financial statements indicate success with the concession?
- Are the sales projection, operational costs and net income statements available?

Grant of right is an exceptionally ideal way for conducting successful marketing when enterprises lack the financial means to market their products or services. In point of fact, assignment of rights enables the company to grow and develop rather rapidly because the assignee bears most of the costs. Actually, this is also the reason for specifying a certain date by which the assignee is supposed to have fulfilled its obligations or else you may terminate the agreement unilaterally. Furthermore, make sure you grant rights to the qualified individuals since your success is interdependent on theirs.

Exports and imports

In general, export companies are relatively small. However, this is one line of activity, which has the potential of opening up many new markets to the business. Of course, it is worth mentioning that export is tedious work because it involves having a complete bearing on the respective domestic and international commerce and trade rules and regulations. Despite this, most governments support export by helping the companies find markets and sales agents in the other countries. The same is also true with regards to import, meaning the governments help and assist the importers in the other countries. in any event, if you intend to get into exports, you have to determine your exact production capacity first. This is done by figuring out the difference between the current production output and the factory's capacity. The commerce and trade procedures and regulations are pretty much the same the world over, and the only thing that could present a challenge is the language barrier and the travels. When the intended the intended export and import markets are determined, certain changes and modifications to the products or services may become necessary.

Competition

Competition occurs both among the enterprises, which offer similar products or services, and also among those that compete for the same customers. Accordingly, a restaurant owner not only competes against other restaurants, but also against sandwich shops, grocers and any other place where customers spend money on food items. The customers reserve the right to pick the place that suits them the most, and it is you who has to give them good enough reasons to come to you. Combine your outstanding ideas with of other people's ideas to give yourself an edge over the competition. Pay attention to the competitions' successes to learn from them and seriously avoid their mistakes and always be ready for change. The tiniest mistake can prove catastrophic to your operations, so you have to have first-hand knowledge of what the competition is doing. Indeed, understanding the competitors can assist you to interpret and view your business environment much better. If you don't know how your competitive edge or strength may react to the plans you have for changing, then your business' workflow is probably inefficient. There are numerous ways through which you can get information on the competition. For example, the suppliers usually have information on the raw materials or semi-constructed parts that their customers buy. Though, they won't share anyone's confidential information, they are always more than willing to talk about their products key features and how their different customers are using them. This type of information should be enough to clue you in on where the competition is standing. In the meantime, don't forget that the competition is trying to find out about you as well. Therefore, being aware of the type of information they are seeking and keeping that information strictly confidential by implementing regulatory standards is of utmost importance.

Participate in the professional meetings held by the entrepreneurs, where novel innovations or new managerial skills may be discussed. Pay particular attention to the successful enterprise ownerships since they typically have excellent information on how to best compete and win in the marketplace. Even though, keeping the competitors away from the business' sensitive information is necessary, in certain instances it can be problematic for your industry or line of work. The competition is bound to react quickly to your business taking the upper hand – something which will lead to destabilization and raise the possibility of problems emerging. One way to avoid the hassle of having to head off the competition is to develop the market for growth. So instead of wasting time and energy fighting your competitors over one customer, concentrate on finding new customers. If you happen to be competing in a market where too many hands are at work like the gas station and restaurant businesses, bring in something new to change the equation to your favor and set yourself apart from all the rest. Moreover, do not attempt to compete directly when a giant company dominates and takes control of the market, and instead try to create products or services that complement theirs. In fact, by offering specially designed products to meet the customer's individual requirements, you may be able to compete with a large corporation. Remember to exclusively concentrate on the areas which the bug company cannot do as well as you. Many entrepreneurs refuse to communicate with their competitors just because they don't like them. However, be smart and avoid these kinds of negative situations and make the business' improvement and progress your number one priority. Furthermore, it might be necessary that you modify certain products or rethink your marketing strategy in order to develop and expand your enterprise. Perhaps, you find it best to produce a series of similar products or turn to complete product diversification. Or you may just want to raise the level quality to not only increase sales to the old customers, but also attract many new ones. Producing a new product, which is not your specialty, particularly by using the existing manufacturing methods, facilities and financial resources, is another way to avoid having to compete. A useful rule of thumb is developing the market is much more beneficially effective than competing against the other companies. So steer clear off the competition, it is not worth the headache.

Be on the lookout for the loyal employees

At least ninety five percent of your success depends on the people that you recruit. At the onset of work, replacement of employees may reach as high as two hundred percent. When trying to decide on the fate of an employee, always ask yourself: 'Would I have hired this person had I known the things that I know now about him?' If your answer is 'no,' the only question that you have to answer is how to get rid of him as quickly as possible. Look for individuals with great attitudes and appealing personalities. Hire those that work hard and you like and enjoy. And above all, look for the kind of individuals, who believe in and are highly committed to what they do. if you make a mistake in recruiting the wrong person, just let them go fast. The fear of hurting an incompetent and inefficient employee's feelings by firing them is one of the main reasons for the small businesses' failure and defeat. So don't let this happen to you.

Don't forget to be humble and modest

The correct application and use of the solutions and methods presented in this book, as well as the positive points existing in

Jalil Tavazo's life will enable you to reach extraordinary success. However, it is important to keep in mind that success can also bring along the seed of destruction. High income makes many people selfish; a negative quality that is extremely damaging. Success, more often than not, leads to false pride and egotistic arrogance. And it can lead to utter madness causing the person to make irrational decisions, which ultimately result in her or his total decimation. Indeed, few are able to handle success and not become captive to unwarranted and futile pride and excessive self-gratification. Vanity is truly man's biggest enemy. What about you? How will you deal with success? You may lose your sense of meek humbleness and become self-conceited and stop seeing yourself the way that others see you. You believe that you are humble and modest, but you are not. And in time, you will begin to make decisions that hurt your future and eventually lead to your demise. Some of the signs indicating the loss of meekness are as follows:

1. Getting angry too quickly.
2. Blowing up at the employees.
3. Assuming an aggressive behavior towards the service people.
4. Ignoring the subordinates..
5. Turning into a spendthrift and spending extravagantly and irresponsibly.
6. Never having time for anyone.
7. Deciding in a certain way to influence the other people.
8. Speaking loudly, so that others can supposedly hear, but

really just to gloat and show off.

9. Exaggerating.

10. Taking credit for anything good.

11. Not being able to take other people's success.

12. Using power in an imposing manner.

13. Expecting others' respect and courtesy and rewarding the subservient or the consummate fawners.

14. Enjoying compliments excessively.

15. Driving away the good people with opposing views.

If you possess any one of these qualities, then you have succumbed and become captive to selfishness. Remember that false pride can readily hurt a person. The way of dealing with the other people is clearly indicative of a sound and healthy state of mind. Unfortunately, success makes many entrepreneurs, athletes and artists egotistical, and they start perceiving themselves to be some sort of a god. They become indifferent and address everybody else angrily and humiliatingly. Conceited attitude has severe consequences, so if you can maintain your humbleness, you have effectively freed yourself of a great deal of unnecessary hardship and pain – something that requires immense attention and effort, but is sure worth the try.

Apply the seven secrets of success

There seven key activities listed below can increase the possibility of achieving great success in your personal life and career:

1. Determine what it is that you want exactly.. The, write it down somewhere and work on it every day.

2. Determine the price that you're willing to pay to reach your goals and decide to pay it. And start immediately.

3. Accept one hundred percent of your responsibilities and what you are now and what you will be in the future. And repeat over and over again: 'If it's going to happen, I have to do it myself.'

4. Be one hundred percent committed to you success and never burn the bridges behind you. Do not ever thing about retreating and keep on reminding yourself that 'defeat is simply not an option.'

5. Be prepared to work hard like you never imagined. And be ready to give way more than what is expected of you and work more than what you actually get paid for since this a key reason for success in your business or professional career.

6. Use every single minute, hour and day wisely. The only thing that you really have to sell is your time, so use it correctly and focus on the most valuable aspects of your work.

7. Support your plans through your strong will and perseverance and decide in advance to never give up and surrender. To persevere is probably the most important character trait that you can create within you in order to guarantee your ultimate success.

Iranian Great Entrepreneur Books are originally created by Great Entrepreneur Institution in Iran and you can access their books in Iran through this here:

www.karafarinanebozorg.com

Also, to access books all around the world click bellow:

www.kidsocado.com/greatentrepreneur

How to access kidsocado Publishing House

www.kidsocado.com/shop

www.ingramcontent.com/pod-product-compliance
Lightning Source LLC
Chambersburg PA
CBHW052206070526
44585CB00017B/2096